Emotional Sigma™

THE 8 STEP PROCESS TO EMOTIONALLY INTELLIGENT LEADERSHIP

Andrew Milivojevich

The Knowledge Management Group Inc
MISSISSAUGA, ONTARIO

The Knowledge Management Group Inc.
1250 Eglinton Avenue West, Unit A12, Suite330
Mississauga, Ontario L5V-1N3

Emotional Sigma/ Andrew Milivojevich. —1st ed.
ISBN 978-0995236301

Contents

This book is dedicated to my wife Antonette and my two boys Michael and Nicholas – I love them dearly!

"The relationships we nurture lead to better outcomes."

—ANDREW MILIVOJEVICH

Emotional Sigma Roadmap

Emotional Sigma

The 8 Step Process to Emotionally Intelligent Leadership
For Executives, Managers, Business Professionals & Team Leaders

To learn more visit:
andrewmilivojevich.com/emotional-sigma

RECOGNIZE
symptoms that suggest positive or negative behavior

DEFINE
emotions that create the desired/undesired state

MEASURE
the consequences of acting on emotions.

CONTROL
emotional outcomes in a positive way

IMPROVE
the current emotional state

ANALYZE
emotional episodes objectively

STANDARDIZE
methods used to manage future emotional episodes

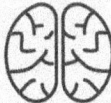

INTEGRATE
emotional lessons into the leadership coaching cycle

ASSESSMENT
WHAT'S YOUR EMOTIONAL SIGMA?

TAKE THE SURVEY!

brough to you by:

#1 andrewmilivojevich.com

1

Emotional Sigma Survey

Take the 5 minute Self-Assessment - It's Free!

https://andrewmilivojevich.com/essbook

Use the Code: essbook

Download Resources

Download Support Documents Used in this Book

https://andrewmilivojevich.com/esdocuments

Forward

I often wonder about the modern workplace. It is a complex environment where people manage, create, operate and conduct a wide variety of activities. Each day is filled with many transactions. Some transactions are in person while others are through media such as e-mail, phone, virtual meetings and face to face activities. While today's workplace strives to build robust and efficient work processes, it often provides limited means to create and strengthen relationships.

Emotional Sigma is a refreshing look at the question of how to build processes for positive relationships in the workplace. The book brings a process approach to making emotional intelligence an essential foundation to set up and sustain healthy relationships within the workplace. It asks the tough question of what could we do to build meaningful relationships. Then, it takes the reader through a stepwise journey of questions, defining the experience and then developing a set of answers for improving relationships. It is this stepwise progression that translates emotional intelligence into an easy journey of discovery for any individual, group or team.

It is said, "small-things come in great packages." *Emotional Sigma* is not a quick read. Instead, it is a road map to self-discovery, insight, and opportunity to pursue meaningful outcomes. Supported by exercises, examples, and an online survey tool, it is the essential start to a journey of extraordinary personal, team and organizational growth.

This book sets the stage for building a system to make today's workplace rich in processes that support personal relationships and enhance service delivery.

Enjoy the adventure.

Jerry Mings

Ethan Jerry Mings is a facilitator, mediator, and quality professional located in Oakville, Ontario. His works specialize in Boards of Directors and Seniors Teams in the private, public and healthcare sector.

The Next Frontier

The industrial landscape, in the United States, is much different today. Many organizations have moved their manufacturing operations overseas. The result; about two-thirds of the jobs in the United States are service based.

Service jobs, unlike manufacturing, are transactional. Such jobs depend on the sharing of information to advance work; hence the reason we refer to them as a transactional process. A distinguishing feature, of a transactional process, is the need for human *interaction* and *intervention*. In this context, an *interaction* occurs when two or more people have an effect upon one another. An *intervention* is a deliberate task performed to an object to advance work.

Take for example the last time you ordered fast food through a drive-thru.

1. *You wait in line, behind another car, and hope your turn comes soon.*

2. *At the Order Kiosk you are greeted by someone that takes, verifies and confirms your order.*

3. *You drive ahead where another person accepts your payment.*

4. *You then drive up to meet another person that hands you your order.*

This may not seem like a complicated process. But consider this. You **interacted** with 3 different people. The first person took your order, the second took your payment, and the third gave you your order.

Let's suppose your fast food order was a hamburger, fries, and pop. Chances are one person made your hamburger. This process required one person working with several food items. Another person got your pop and fries. This type of work is typical of the work seen in manufacturing. Here people performed several tasks using various objects to complete a job. In these cases, deliberate tasks performed to objects to complete a job are an example of human **intervention**.

Transactional processes often include human intervention and interaction. In the case of our fast food order, human interaction is critical to communicate an order and process payment.

Suppose the verbal exchange was unpleasant. How would that affect your experience? Would you consider placing a future order with that establishment? The truth is you might consider taking your business elsewhere! There is a lot of research that confirms the link between customer satisfaction and behavioral intentions.

Suppose you brushed off that unpleasant verbal exchange to find that it happens again and again. A continued sense of poor customer satisfaction will lead to specific behavioral intentions. Such intentions result in finding another place to take your business. Losing one customer may not be a big deal. But what if this experience is typical? Imagine all the lost business!

The face of Continuous Improvement is changing. The last 100 years was about tools and techniques to reduce variation in products and processes. Today the nature of work is somewhat different - there are more and more transactional processes. That means we've got more people interacting with each other. Therefore, knowing how to interact with other people is critical. Human interactions that result in negative behavioral intentions will kill any business. Thus, reducing the variation in human behavior is the next frontier. *Emotional Sigma* uses the systematic approach of Six Sigma to improve Emotional Intelligence. Using this approach, people can learn how to improve human behavior and drive positive business outcomes.

Andrew Milivojevich
P.Eng., M.Sc., ASQ Fellow

Preface

When you work with as many Six Sigma change agents as I have, you tend to see things that will determine which Six Sigma candidates are successful and which are not. In my early days, as a Six Sigma practitioner, I would identify Six Sigma candidates based on their ability to acquire and apply knowledge to create innovative solutions for a vast number of manufacturing and service problems. However, for some unknown reason, some projects were completed faster while others took way too long to finish. During a number of post project review sessions, I would continuously seek to know why projects took so long to complete. Over time, I got a number of responses to my question. Some of them I'll share with you in the list below.

"My team members were not up to the challenge."

"Management failed to respond to my complaints about this project."

"This project requires too many resources not wanting to contribute."

"The team leader does no work and takes all the credit."

"This guy is only interested in self-promotion not the interests of the team.".

I could go on, but I think you get the idea. As an engineer, statistician and scientist I realized I needed to unravel the circumstances perpetrating the responses I witnessed in an effort to isolate the root cause(s). Therefore, to formulate a hypothesis, I consolidated the observations from successful projects as communicated to me by Six Sigma Black Belt candidates. The following is a sample of the comments I received.

"I had a great team. It was a pleasure working with everyone."

"I can't wait to work with this team again."

"I never had so much fun."

"I learned an enormous amount and was able to share and discover how other departments operate."

By comparing the two sets of remarks one can see a common element. One group of participants had difficulty with resources while the other did not. I started asking myself why one group had problems while the other did not. I searched for something that was different between the groups. Eventually, I realized that the issue was not with the scope of the project, the training people received or the fact some Six Sigma candidates were doing their regular jobs. The issue actually came down to the people themselves.

In the 1980's the concept of emotional intelligence began to take shape. During this time, studies began to reveal startling facts. A series of studies at Yale University showed a link between emotional intelligence and personal achievement, happiness, and professional success[1]. Such studies began to suggest and explain why people of the same cognitive intellect could have different levels of success. To date, there is no known connection between cognitive intelligence and emotional intelligence.

Do emotions in the workplace matter? There is a multitude of research studies that suggest emotions do matter. Some research studies suggest that how managers "feel" is a helpful indicator and predictor of organizational performance. One particular research study demonstrates that how a management team "feels" significantly impacts a company's earnings[2].

Could the emotional disposition within a group contribute to the success of a project or potentially delay it so that it takes too long to complete? There are a number of research studies that address this specific question. One in particular is interesting. In this research study[3], two teams were created. The first team was made up of members high in emotional intelligence while the other team consisted of members low in emotional intelligence. Both teams were able to complete their respective assignments. However, the team high in emotional intelligence had better performance during the first weeks of the investigation. Essentially, the team high in emotional intelligence was able to perform in a manner that got the job done in a more efficient way. Alternatively, the team low in emotional intelligence eventually did catch up to the team high in emotional intelligence but at the expense of lost productivity and hundreds of worker hours.

Ultimately, emotions do affect team performance and can have a powerful impact. Therefore, being aware of the impact emotions can have on human performance in the workplace is critical. How people in a team "feel" can influence individual and team performance in a positive or negative manner. Our job, as change agents, is to understand the emotional dynamics within ourselves and among other people so that such emotions can be used to improve leadership and human performance in the workplace.

This book is the continuous exploration and discovery into the role of emotional intelligence applied within framework of Six Sigma to improve the leadership capabilities of people at all levels within the organization. It seeks to improve leadership and human performance in the workplace in a systematic manner using the Emotional Sigma model for breakthrough improvement in Emotional Intelligence.

I welcome comments from my readers -- thoughts, suggestions, stories, reflections. While I cannot respond to all emails, I would be happy to hear from you.

Andrew Milivojevich
andrew@andrewmilivojevich.com

Introduction

L eaders and employees alike often work within a team environment to accomplish projects in an effort to achieve a desired objective. In most cases, team members have job duties outside the project and report directly to other managers. This often means that team members may find that their services are required elsewhere within the organization. Given this reality Team Leaders must motivate, manage and guide their teams to success in the face of competing demands on team members' time. Ultimately, Team Leaders must use human resources effectively and ensure that time is not wasted because of poor team dynamics.

Leaders must guide, manage, and motivate teams to accomplish assignments. To this end, Emotional Intelligence (EI) is a useful leadership skill that can significantly improve team performance. When EI is practiced successfully, it can yield results in a shorter period of time. This was observed by Jordan et al., who found that the high EI teams were able to get organized quicker and were more productive, thereby saving time that would have been lost had EI not been practiced.

When projects have tight timelines, Team Leaders must form strong teams quickly, communicate goals; and obtain commitment from team members, regardless of reporting structure. Within this environment, Team Leaders must lead by using highly sophisticated skills that involve understanding how people think and feel. In other words, Team Leaders must be Emotionally Intelligent Observers and Practitioners.

CHAPTER ONE

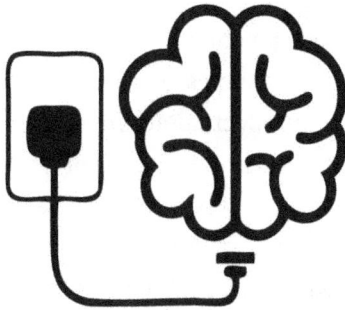

Emotional Intelligence

Intellect and emotions

At present there does not appear to be a link between intellectual and emotional intelligence. They appear to be mutually exclusive as shown in Figure 1. The intellectual disposition of a person does not predict whether he or she is emotionally intelligent. Conversely, that a person is high in emotional intelligence does not predict whether that same person is intelligent.

Have you ever had the pleasure of knowing an absolutely brilliant person with whom you could not get along? In my corporate experience I have had the pleasure of working with some of the most brilliant people I have ever met. Some of them were an inspiration to me, and I acquired an enormous amount of technical knowledge from them. Given their brilliance, however, they never climbed the corporate ladder and in many instances were assigned roles and responsibilities inconsistent with their intellectual abilities. Eventually, these brilliant people were left in low level positions, not responsible for directing cross functional teams or interacting with senior management. In some instances these people were asked to leave the company. These brilliant individuals lacked the emotional intelligence to deal with the diverse emotions that go with certain jobs. Their intellect was not in question; rather their ability to work constructively with cross-functional teams and senior management was. Ultimately, how smart a person is does not predict how far he or she will advance up the corporate ladder.

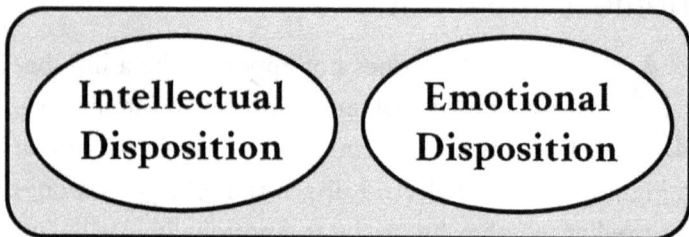

Intellectual Disposition — Emotional Disposition

Figure 1: Intellect & Emotions are mutually exclusive

During my consulting career, I had the pleasure of working with a shop floor supervisor. He was selected for Six Sigma Black Belt training. Initially, I had some reservations about his ability to comprehend the material. However, I underestimated his passion to fix a host of problems using Six Sigma tools and his ability to interact with other people to drive projects. During his training, he sought out knowledgeable people to supplement his coaching in an effort to learn the Six Sigma material. During his project, he built strong relationships with people, completed his project and successfully achieved Black Belt certification. This individual was one of the best Black Belts I have ever coached. This person did not realize it, and neither did I at the time, but his aptitude to manage his own emotions and work with other people demonstrated a high degree of emotional intelligence. His experience was acquired through years of managing people on the shop floor. In the end, even though this person only had a high school education, he was able to use his emotional intelligence to leverage resources to help improve his intellectual disposition and complete many successful projects.

Emotions affect how we work in teams

Emotions may be used to enhance our thinking. They can influence thinking in a manner that increases our ability to reason and to problem-solve, both of which are important in a team environment. In the book Primal Leadership, Daniel Goleman et.al. states that "feeling good lubricates mental efficiency[5]." Essentially, feeling good enhances our ability to process complex information effectively while we remain flexible in making decisions. Team Leaders must pay attention to the dynamics and the emotional environment within a group if they are to use emotions in a manner that establishes and sustains a positive atmosphere. Doing so will enable the team to come up with innovative solutions and complete projects in a timely manner.

As noted by neuroscientist Antonio Damasio, "Appropriate emotions speed up the decision-making enormously[6]." This was demonstrated in a study by Carlos Estrada, Alice Isen, and Mark Young where medical practitioners were given small gifts as a means of altering their moods. The research found that participants made diagnoses that were both faster and more accurate after they were given the gifts[7]. In another study, Sigal Barsade et. al. demonstrated that how a management team feels can directly affect a company's bottom-line. Results showed that a top management team sharing a positive emotional outlook will have four to six percent higher market-adjusted earnings per share than companies whose management teams hold diverse emotional outlooks[8].

These studies suggest that emotions do affect our behavior and ability to reason. Specifically, when individuals experience a positive emotion such as happiness, they are better at generating solutions to a problem. Essentially, positive moods tend to increase decision-making abilities[9].

Other emotions, such as mild anxiety or fear, can motivate team members to re-check their assumptions. Used effectively and in the correct context, mild fear may be a powerful emotion when used positively. However, intense fear can paralyze and immobilize individuals and negatively affect the performance of a team.

Elements of Emotional Intelligence

As illustrated in Figure 2, Emotional Intelligence (EI) may be partitioned into four categories: self-awareness,

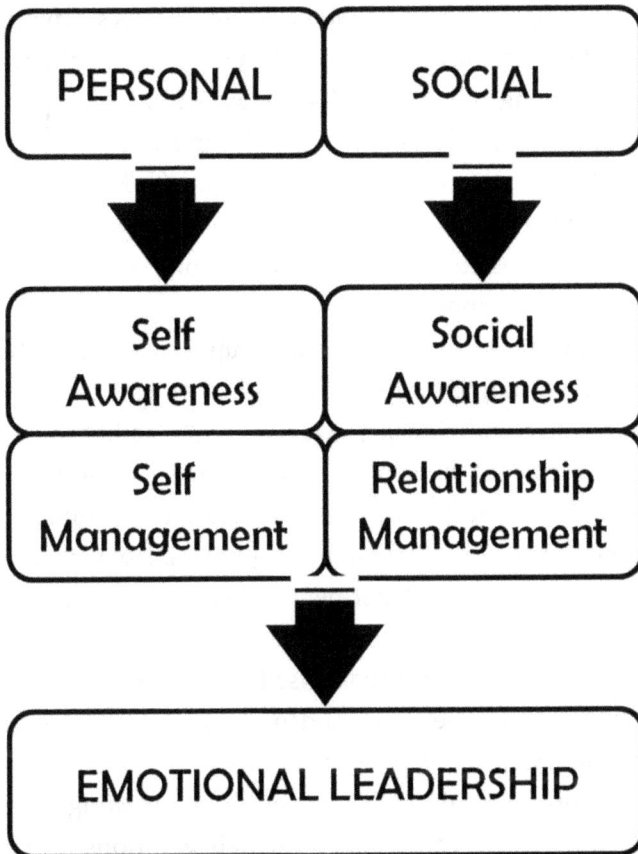

Figure 2: Categories of Emotions Intelligence

self-management, social awareness, and relationship management[10]. *Self-awareness* and *self-management* describe *personal competencies*, while *social awareness* and *relationship management* deal with *social competencies.*

Personal and Social Competencies Explained

Self-awareness refers to the ability of an individual to acknowledge their precise emotions and remain aware of them as they occur. *Self-management* involves remaining flexible and directing one's behavior positively as a result of being self-aware. *Social awareness* is observing emotions accurately in other people, and understanding what they are thinking and feeling. Finally, *Relationship Management* is the ability of an individual to use their awareness of their own and other people's emotions to manage interactions effectively.

Self-awareness is the foundation upon which the other EI traits may be improved. When tuned into their own feelings, individuals possess a unique ability to perceive the current environment in which they find themselves. Since the environment provides the stimulus, a person who is *self-aware* can begin to recognize how such a stimulus may affect other people within the same environment, thereby promoting *social awareness.*

When individuals become self-aware they begin to realize how their behavior and/or what they say can affect other people. They evaluate how they should act or what should be said consistent with the existing environment. Doing so assures that their emotions do not control them, thus improving *self- management.* Subsequently, individuals begin to see the behavior of others through another lens. They are more thoughtful of other people and their actions thus improving *social awareness*. These individuals become more comfortable taking an active role in understanding the circumstances and emotional elements affecting other people positively, hence improving their *relationship management* skills. Individuals who inherently use these four emotional intelligence qualities exude positive behaviors that resonate with other people and foster an environment of loyalty. In the end, leadership is both given and earned. The path to leadership and emotional stability may be improved by using, in a systematic manner, the **Emotional Sigma** model described in this book.

How we process emotions

In his book, Emotional Intelligence: why it can matter more than IQ[11], Goleman explains that the environment around us is filled with a plethora of visual stimuli. In Figure 3, visual stimuli enter the retina and go to the thalamus. It is here that visual stimuli are translated into signals that proceed to the visual cortex, where they are assessed and responded to accordingly. Environmental stimuli that are emotional in nature follow two different pathways: a large portion goes to the thalamus then to the visual cortex and finally to the amygdala. However, a small portion bypasses the visual cortex and goes directly from the thalamus to the amygdala. Essentially, the signal is partitioned at the thalamus. Since a small portion of the signal bypasses the visual cortex, any opportunity

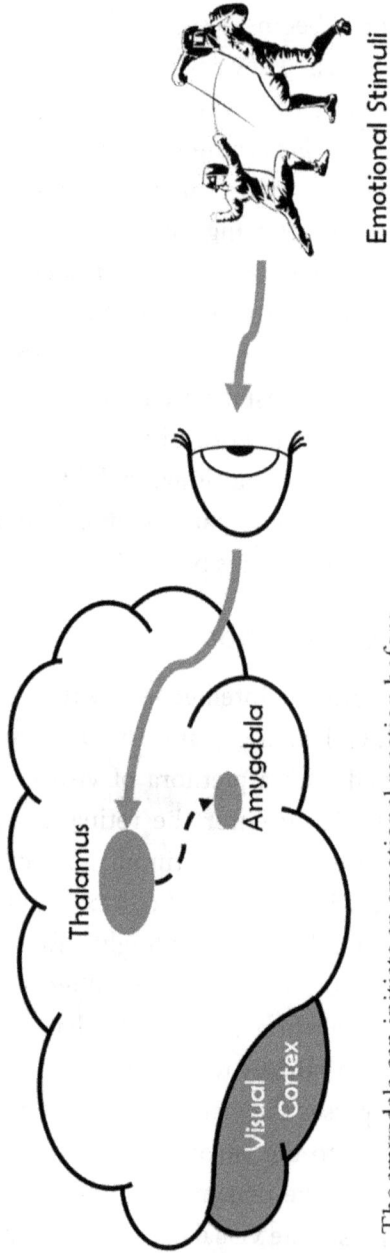

The amygdala can initiate an emotional reaction before the cortical centers can comprehend what is going on.

Figure 3: Understanding how we process emotions

to understand it is lost. Instead, the signal goes straight to the amygdala, the center of many emotional processes, and a response based on less precise information is formulated since the message from the visual cortex has yet to catch up. Therefore, when a stimulus creates a signal that bypasses the visual cortex, an emotional reaction typically ensues. Such a reaction can positively or negatively affect the performance of an individual and affect members of the team. The challenge for Team Leaders is to understand the emotional dynamics that exist within themselves and a team environment. Through such comprehension and the application of *Emotional Sigma*, Team Leaders can effectively use emotions to increase team performance.

Recognizing emotions

Self-awareness is a critical step for Team Leaders who must be emotionally aware so that they can direct themselves in a more productive manner. The first step in self-awareness is to understand how various stimuli are internalized. As shown in Table 1, we react to stimuli in specific and predictable patterns[12]. For example, happiness is associated with slow breathing, a slightly increased heart rate, relaxed muscles, warm body temperature, and sensations localized in the chest area. Alternatively, anger produces shallow breathing, an increased heart rate, a tense jaw, raised body temperature, and sensations throughout the entire body. Understanding how each of these emotions is experienced in our bodies can provide an early warning to an event that may

Emotion	Sensations				
	Breathing	Heart Rate	Muscles	Temperature	Location
Fear	Increases	Increases	Tense	Cold	Abdomen
Anger	Shallow	Increases	Jaw Tense	Hot	Body
Sadness	Deeper	Slows	Relaxed	Cold	Chest
Happiness	Slow	Increases Slightly	Relaxed	Warm	Chest

Table 1: Emotions and corresponding sensations

affect the team or any member, positively or negatively, in our working environment.

If used in the appropriate context, each of the four emotions listed in Table 1 can bring about desired outcomes in group behavior. Note that the emotions presented here are neither exhaustive nor mutually exclusive. They are used for illustration purposes only.

The influence of one's life history

Our past experiences shape our current behavior, including the responses we have in our daily work environment. Consider the following example.

During a corporate initiative, a Team Leader encountered a situation that could have resulted in a dysfunctional group had **Emotional Sigma** not been practiced. The Team Leader had bonded with the other members of the team and gained their trust and respect. A few team members, troubled by a recent experience with management, shared their concerns with the Team Leader. The Team Leader concluded that the best interests of the team members had been compromised and that they were being victimized and exploited. He arrived at this conclusion based on past experiences. At a young age, he formed a strong belief that victimization and exploitation were immoral and should not be tolerated. Consequently, he was sympathetic to the team members and moved to anger. The emotionally intelligent Team Leader recognized that his sensations; shallow breathing, increased heart rate, tense jaw, and hot body temperature might result in behavior disruptive to the group, no matter how well intentioned. Instead, the Team Leader sought to become emotionally positive and brought up his concerns with management in a more constructive manner.

A strong scientific disposition was part of the Team Leader's life history. Once he became aware of his emotions, he could draw on his experience to ask questions in order to acquire more information about the concerns identified by the team members. In the end, he was able to make an informed judgment and remain emotionally committed to the success of the team and the overall corporate initiative, as well as fulfilling management expectations and achieving corporate goals.

Had the Team Leader approached management from a position of anger, the resulting discussions would have been explosive and barriers to the success of the corporate initiative may have resulted.

Observing emotional behavior in others

Once we become self-aware, our focus shifts to becoming socially aware. That is, how can we recognize emotions in someone else we feel ourselves? Since we cannot directly feel the sensations others experience, we must learn to recognize them visually. Much research has been done in this area. Facial expressions, body posture, and tone of voice can communicate the emotions people may be feeling. In Figure 4, we show the various facial expressions that describe happiness, fear, sadness, and anger[13].

Happiness   Fear

Sadness   Anger

Figure 4: Basic emotional expressions

In Table 2, we show the types of body posture and describe what these nonverbal cues suggest emotionally[14]. In Table 3, the various types of emotions are described versus tone of voice[15].

Non-verbal cues speak loudly

During a corporate initiative, a meeting was called by a Team Leader assigned to guide the efforts of a group.

BODY POSTURE	WHAT IT LOOKS LIKE	WHAT IT SUGESTS
Orientation	Facing towards you	Interest
	Turned away	Closed off
Arms	Arms open	Openness
	Arms folded	Defensiveness
Posture	Leaning forward	Interest
	Leaning away from you	Rejection

Table 2: Non-verbal cues

Tone of Voice & Emotions

Speech Tone	Emotion
Monotone	Boredom
Slow speed & pitch	Depression
High speed, empathetic pitch	Enthusiasm
Ascending tone	Surprise
Abrupt speech	Defensiveness
Terse, loud tone	Anger
High pitch, drawn-out speech	Disbelief

Table 3: Tone of voice

The Team Leader sought a status update for each project being managed. It should be noted that the Team Leader was specifically selected for this role because of his experience and ability to work effectively with people. Through years of experience the Team Leader had learned to recognize group behaviors that would produce positive or negative outcomes. Essentially, he was skilled at social awareness and utilized the information to manage relationships effectively.

At the start of the meeting, the Team Leader noticed a number of nonverbal cues indicating defensiveness and rejection from team members. Before beginning, the Team Leader addressed the emotions exhibited by the group. Rather than asking for status updates, the Team Leader asked team members to describe their experiences with the corporate initiative. It became clear that they were experiencing strong negative emotions -- namely, fear and anger. The team members revealed that they were still performing their regular duties and could not find the time to complete their projects. The Team Leader knew management would not reverse its decision to keep team members in their current jobs. However, if the team members could not complete their projects, the corporate initiative would fail. Team members would be demoralized, improvement goals set out in the strategic plan would not be realized, and the bottom-line would be adversely affected.

Upon further investigation, the Team Leader discovered that the root cause of the negative emotions was not a lack of support from the business unit managers. Rather, new product lines had been introduced that required much of the team members' attention.

The Team Leader chose to instill a sense of shared purpose among the group to address their concerns. He asked for possible suggestions that might free up time for the team members while insuring that the new product launches were not compromised. Once suggestions were identified, the Team Leader and the team members selected their top two choices.

A meeting was called with the leadership group responsible for operations. The team communicated their concerns and highlighted solutions that would reduce potential risks. The solutions were well received and implemented. During the regularly scheduled project review sessions, the Team Leader monitored project progression to make sure that the solutions sufficiently addressed the root problem. The Team Leader documented the experiences and communicated the lessons learned.

CHAPTER TWO

Emotional Sigma
THE 8 STEP PROCESS TO
EMOTIONALLY INTELLIGENT LEADERSHIP

A brief overview of the process

Emotions may be visualized as an abstract mathe-matical equation[16]. If the episode "f" causes "X" to occur, the effect is the observed emotion "Y." By thinking of emotions from this point of view, we may develop a methodology that seeks to address emotions in a scientific manner. Table 4 presents the Emotional Sigma Process, an eight-step process that may be used to deal with emotions in the workplace.

The first step requires that we *recognize* the symp-toms which suggest positive and/or negative behavior. The second step requires that we *define* the emotion(s) creating the desired/undesired state. The third step de-mands that we *measure* the consequence of the emo-tion(s). The fourth step insists that we *analyze* the episode(s) and identify the root cause(s) creating emo-tional instability. The fifth step compels us to implement and validate solutions that *improve* the current emotional state by addressing the circumstance(s) causing emotional instability. The sixth step expects that we will monitor and sustain solutions that *control* our emotional instability. The seventh step, expects that having learned from our experience we will *standardize* and document the methods used to address the circumstance(s) causing emotional instability. Finally, in step eight we must *integrate* the lessons learned from the previous step, into the Leadership coaching cycle.

Emotional Sigma may be employed on an individual level or within the context of a group, leadership team, or organization. When executed properly, it addresses episodes and emotions causing dysfunctional individuals, teams, and organizations. *Emotional Sigma* may also be employed as a methodology for improving overall emotional wellness for all employees. It is a disciplined methodology that views emotions from a scientific perspective. Through such a perspective, we can learn from our emotions, substantially increase our emotional intelligence, and realize a host of benefits for both the individual and the organization.

Emotional Sigma | The 8 Step Process to Emotionally Intelligent Leadership

Process Step	Objective
Recognize	the 'Symptoms' that suggest positive or negative behavior
Define	emotions that creates the desired or undesired state
Measure	the consequence of acting on emotions
Analyze	emotional episodes objectively
Improve	the current emotional state
Control	emotional outcomes in a positive way
Standardize	methods used to manage future emotional episodes
Integrate	emotional lessons into the leadership coaching cycle.

Table 4: Emotional Sigma Process

CHAPTER THREE

Recognize

Recognize the physical signs of emotional behavior

Each of us is exposed to a number of stimuli. Such stimuli can be visual, auditory, physical contact or a combination thereof. Recognizing how these stimuli affect us and what emotional reactions they stimulate in us are important first steps to improving our self-awareness and personal competency. We perceive various stimuli in a manner that motivates biological actions within the human body. Our breathing may become slow, deep, rapid or shallow depending on the stimuli we are experiencing. Our muscles can become tense or relaxed. These sensations can also be localized to a specific location on the body such as our back, shoulders or jaw. We may find that our heart rate increases or decreases depending on what we may be experiencing. Alternatively, we may find that our body temperature increases and we begin to sweat all over or it is localized to the palms of our hands, brow, or forehead. We may begin to feel a flush and the sensation is localized in our face. If the sensation is strong, our face may become red.

Try to visualize the following situation. Assume that your long lost sweetheart is standing next to you. The two of you are alone; there is nobody else around. Just imagine the moment. You finally have an opportunity to express your true feelings! Your heart pounds like crazy, your hands get clammy, and you start to breathe faster. At this moment, the intensity of your body's biological response and the subsequent number of potential emotions stimulated by such biological actions is enormous. Your emotions are internalized; they have yet to explode externally. You are still standing next to that very special person and you have yet to say a word. You look just as normal as anyone else.

You understand the relationship between the way your body reacts and how your emotions can be connected to a physical action within your body. Your quick heartbeat, clammy hands, and the shortness of breath are biological actions associated with the emotion called fear.

Fear is an emotion that has us question everything we do. You might hesitate starting a conversation with that special someone out of fear that you might trip over each word and embarrass yourself. If this emotion gets the better part of you, you may have lost an opportunity to live out the rest of your life in sheer happiness or not – you will never know.

The intensity of an emotion is directly related to the intensity of its corresponding biological actions. The more we feel our body responding, the greater the intensity of the emotion. To improve our self-awareness we must train ourselves to interpret our body's signals appropriately. We must understand our biological actions, the emotions that ensue, and whether or not the emotion motivates positive or negative behavior.

Exercise

The next time you find yourself interacting with others, try to assess your current state. Specifically, pay special attention to the following:

1. Is your breathing normal, slow, fast, shallow, and deep?

2. Are your muscles tense or relaxed? Where is the sensation localized?

3. Is your heart rate normal or racing? Do you feel your heart pounding?

4. Do you feel hot? Is the sensation localized to a specific region of the body? Are you sweating?

5. *Are your thoughts racing? Is it hard to pay attention to the environment you currently find yourself in?*

Be sure to write down your experiences and keep a log. Over time, you can examine your log and look for patterns and trends in your own biological reactions to various situations.

CHAPTER FOUR

Define

Define the emotions creating the behavior

Biological actions precede emotions. To improve our emotional intelligence, we need to become self-aware of what our bodies are telling us. In this manner, we can develop an early warning mechanism that seeks to provide sufficient warning as to potential emotions triggered by such biological actions that might produce positive or negative behaviors.

There are five basic emotions. They are Happiness, Sadness, Anger, Fear, and Shame[17]. These basic emotions have degrees of intensity. As such, different words may be used to describe your experience of "happiness."

For example, Table 5 shows that being "pleased" or "thrilled" are emotions that may be grouped under the general emotional category of "happiness." However, each emotion differs in intensity. "Pleased" and "thrilled" are either mild or intense emotions associated with happiness. Use a word that best describes the intensity of the emotion you are experiencing and has more meaning for you. It is important to understand which emotion you experience most often and the intensity. Over time, you can determine which of the five basic emotions you tend to experience and the degree to which you experience it.

As you become familiar with your own biological actions correlated with the various emotions you experience, you will need to label them in a manner that makes sense to you. Once you identify the biological actions and name the related emotion(s), you can start to map their relationships. It will take time, but will be a valuable exercise that will go a long way towards improving your overall self-awareness and emotional intelligence.

Once you become familiar with your emotional vocabulary, you will be able to link those emotions occurring most often to specific biological actions. Then you will be on your way to increasing your self-awareness, improving your personal competency and utilizing emotional intelligence.

To use Table 5 effectively, try to identify which of the five major emotions you are experiencing and determine its intensity. For example, suppose you are experiencing an intense emotion within the emotional category "fear".

You may choose to select "terrified" as the word that best describes your emotional intensity. By using the following table, over time, you can collect an enormous amount of data. With such data, you can determine the frequency of the emotion experienced the most and cross reference it to the corresponding emotional category and intensity. This will provide a measure of your emotional intelligence. With such a measure, a specific training protocol can be developed that will address your specific emotional performance. With training, you can increase your emotional performance by working on those specific emotions affecting you on a frequent basis. Recognizing biological signals and defining emotions are critical steps to increasing self-awareness and improving personal competency.

Can positive or negative emotions have negative and positive consequences?

Each of the emotions listed in Table 5 can be used beneficially in the correct context. For example, "fear" is a strong emotion that can be used positively while "happiness" can have negative consequences. Consider the following example.

Imagine a group of individuals assigned to work on a particular proposal. The team leader is confident that she has an "exuberant" team who work well with each other. They have met challenges in the past and have succeeded each time. They believe that they can handle

Intensity	EMOTION				
	Happiness	Sadness	Anger	Fear	Shame
High	Elated	Depressed	Furious	Terrified	Sorrowful
	Excited	Disappointed	Enraged	Horrified	Remorseful
	Overjoyed	Alone	Outraged	Scared Stiff	Unworthy
	Thrilled	Hurt	Aggravated	Petrified	Disgraced
	Exuberant	Dejected	Irate	Fearful	Dishonored
	Ecstatic	Hopeless	Seething	Panicky	
	Fired Up	Sorrowful			
	Delighted	Miserable			
Moderate	Cheerful	Heartbroken	Upset	Scared	Apologetic
	Up	Down	Mad	Frightened	Defamed
	Good	Upset	Hot	Threatened	Sneaky
	Relieved	Distressed	Frustrated	Insecure	Guilty
	Satisfied	Regretful	Agitated	Uneasy	
		Melancholy	Disgusted	Shocked	
Mild	Glad	Unhappy	Perturbed	Apprehensive	Embarrassed
	Contented	Moody	Annoyed	Nervous	Disappointed
	pleasant	Blue	Uptight	Worried	Let Down
	Fine	Lost	Put out	Timid	
	Pleased	Bad	Irritated	Unsure	
		Dissatisfied	Touchy	Anxious	

Table 5: Various expressions of emotions

any challenge. This group exercises high levels of emotional intelligence; their personal and social competencies are exceptional. Their ability to work well together and their success can be directly attributed to the level of "happiness" experienced within the group. Everyone loves their job and the people they interact with. They have created professional relationships and know how to settle differences. They share common goals and objectives and understand their relationship to such goals and objectives. This exceptional team has been assigned to work on a particular proposal.

This proposal, if accepted, will fulfill an important growth strategy for the company. It is the company's first opportunity to do work in a market segment it has been trying to penetrate. To that end, management has informed the team leader to do whatever possible to insure they receive the winning bid while maintaining a mild profit. The team leader is confident, as is her team.

Given their level of "exuberance" and subsequent "happiness" the team leader wonders if it might work against them and cause someone to overlook something that might jeopardize their ability to turn a mild profit. In the past, they could afford to make mistakes since they had a captive market and profits were high. With that in mind, the team leader calls a meeting to explain the importance of winning this bid with a mild profit. This creates a challenge so she communicates that there is no room for error. She instills a modest level of "fear," particularly "apprehension," to motivate the group to recheck their numbers and assumptions, given so much is at stake. The team cannot afford to make a mistake since the profit margin is low.

In this case, mild fear is used as a positive emotion that seeks to reduce any over-confidence that is a consequence of the level of exuberance and subsequent happiness that might exist in the group. In this case, fear is used as a motivator to challenge the group members to re-check their work.

Why maintain an Emotional Sigma journal?

An EI journal is meant to deepen your insight into your life's daily experience. It helps capture all the episodes and events that surround and affect you. An EI journal can provide a detailed record to assist you in the recollection of events and episodes and your response to such events and episodes. Be sure to write down your experiences and keep a log. Over time, you can examine your log and look for patterns and trends in your own biological reactions to various situations.

As part of the coaching process keep in mind that you are attempting to develop your leadership skills and enhance human performance in the workplace by engaging the Emotional Sigma process discussed in this book. As you become more and more familiar with using this strategy, you will begin to recognize new behaviors you employ in the workplace and how others perceive them.

Exercise

The next time you are in a meeting, keep a log of what you are experiencing. Specifically, if you experience a particularly strong emotion, try to give that emotion a name and then identify what biological actions you may have been experiencing just before the emotion was manifested.

Using Table 6, identify the setting and environment in which you find yourself. For example, are you interacting directly or indirectly with a group of other people? This occurs in situations where you find yourself in a meeting room having direct, face to face conversations or meeting with other people in an indirect manner via a video conference or internet session. Using the concepts of "direct" or "indirect" is a way to distinguish the type of interaction taking place between people. Next, determine if the setting is one where you are alone, having an emotional moment as a consequence of reflecting on your own thoughts or reading a report or memo. Once you have defined the setting, take stock of your biological actions when you experience the emotion. Finally, isolate the emotion and define its intensity. Once you have a sufficient catalog of experiences, you will have defined your emotions and the biological actions motivating such emotions. From this, you can formulate a plan that may be used to increase your emotional intelligence.

Incident Recording Sheet

Name: _____   Date: _____

Describe the Episode/Event: _____

_____

_____

Episode/ Event	Biological Actions	Feeling	Emotional Consequences
In Group	**Breathing**	**Emotion**	**Notes:**
☐ Direct	☐ Slow	☐ Happiness	
☐ Indirect	☐ Normal	☐ Sadness	
One on One	☐ Fast	☐ Anger	
☐ Direct	☐ Shallow	☐ Fear	
☐ Indirect	☐ Deep	☐ Shame	
Alone	**Muscles**	**Intensity**	
☐ Direct	☐ Relaxed	☐ High	
☐ Indirect	☐ Tense	Name:	
Stimuli	**Heart Rate**		
_____	☐ Slow	☐ Medium	
_____	☐ Normal	Name:	
_____	☐ Racing		
_____	☐ Pounding	☐ Low	
	Temperature	Name:	
_____	☐ Cold		
_____	☐ Normal		
_____	☐ Hot		
	☐ Sweating		

Table 6: Incident recording sheet

CHAPTER FIVE

Measure

Measure the consequence of emotions

Once we recognize and define the biological actions associated to specific emotions we can judge how such emotions, if expressed, will be perceived by others. We need to train ourselves in a manner that will effectively measure the consequence of those emotions expressed in our daily interactions with people, thereby improving "self-management". By first recognizing our own physical signs, then defining emotions and finally understanding the relationship between the two, we can direct our behavior in a positive manner.

To a large degree, our past experiences shape our behavior. At this point it is important to recall your own life history. To measure the consequence of your emotions successfully, you need to understand what events in your life had a profound effect on you.

For example, as a teenager, you may have had a parent who required your help with the chores around the house. During such chores, your friends may have gone to the movies without you because you were always helping out at home. As a result, you may have resented the restrictions on your personal freedom as a consequence of having to perform such chores. If this was a recurring experience, you may have developed a strong belief that restricting one's personal freedom is wrong.

Assume for a moment you are no longer a teenager, but an adult in the corporate world, that is repeatedly asked to work late. Based on your life history, you might begin to feel a mild, moderate, or intense emotion associated with "anger". If you do not consider the consequence of your emotion, you might affect your relationship with your boss that could have a lasting negative effect.

Since we do not ultimately know how people may react, try to use your best judgment. In most cases, you need to ask yourself how you would feel if you were on the receiving end of a positive or negative emotional reaction. Remember that what is important is the desired response you wish to achieve. Either a positive or negative emotion can achieve that response.

We tend to act on our emotions without thinking about the consequences. If you find yourself acting on emotion, remember that it may lack "reason". If such emotions motivate you into action without first considering what the consequences are, you may find yourself in a situation without understanding why you did what you did.

When you sense a biological action, take immediate notice because a potential undesired emotion maybe around the corner. If revealed, it can have an enormous impact on the immediate group of people with whom you are interacting.

I like to practice a simple technique that makes me put some thought into how I wish to guide my actions. Specifically, I like to "stop", "breathe", "think" and if necessary "channel".

If you find yourself experiencing a biological action, such as a flush sensation localized too your forehead as well as a tense jaw, you may be experiencing "anger". If this emotion takes over, based on your life history you may react by losing emotional control. You now need to think about the consequences of that kind of behavior. You need to consider whether such an outburst is appropriate for the environment in which you find yourself. If that environment is a meeting where the objective is to resolve a customer concern, you would be best to refrain from such an outburst. Otherwise, you risk your relationship with the customer, and the consequences could be dire.

Alternatively, if the environment is a sports event and you are feeling annoyed that your team is losing the game, it might be appropriate to show your disappointment by shouting a mild insult to the referee who made a bad call or a football player who dropped the ball in the end zone.

When in a professional setting, if you believe the outburst will have an undesired impact, you may need to "channel" this energy until you can effectively calm down and collect your thoughts. You need to find an appropriate method to "channel" undesired emotions.

When I "channel" I like to write my thoughts on a word processor. Such an activity forces me to exercise my scientific disposition by articulating my thoughts enough to release my emotional baggage, thereby returning me to a point where I can think objectively. This usually works in specific situations. In other cases, when people find themselves in situations where their emotions are getting the better of them, some people will admit it and remove themselves from such situations until they return to objectivity.

Exercise

Reflect upon a couple of experiences, both bad and good, for which you were recently responsible. Recall the emotions that were in effect and ask yourself whether you could predict, with certainty, the consequence of those experiences. Try to capture both experiences using Table 6. For that experience to have gone differently, what could you have done differently? If that emotional experience was strong, how could you have channeled your emotions?

CHAPTER SIX

Analyze

Analyze the episodes and identify the root cause(s) of emotional behavior

When we find that a particular stimulus motivates certain biological actions relating to a particular emotion, and that emotion is strong enough to displace reason, we need to be "self-aware" that it is happening. We need to measure its consequence and use such information to "self-manage" our behavior in an effective manner. This chain of events is illustrated in Figure 5.

To analyze this chain of events effectively, we need to understand the circumstance generating the stimulus. Understanding the circumstance helps identify the root-cause triggering the emotion. Consider the following scenario.

Rob is an executive responsible for business process improvement for a large organization. While returning from a meeting, Rob receives a phone call from Dan, one of his project managers. During the conversation Dan communicates his frustration with another executive - Jim. Jim is responsible for operations and provides direction for a number of initiatives being deployed throughout the organization. Essentially, Jim is spending an unusual amount of time off-site. Therefore, Jim cannot attend regularly scheduled meetings to provide the appropriate sign-offs. He has also failed to return a number of phone calls from Dan. This has continued for a couple weeks. Dan, overcome with frustration, begins to speak in a manner making it clear that his previously strong and positive opinions of Jim are being replaced with doubt and an increased sense of frustration with him. Dan also communicates that other members of the organization have noticed Jim's lack of attendance and are beginning to question what is going on. Dan is beginning to believe that Jim does not support his project initiative. Rob, being responsible for business process improvement, realizes that timelines will be affected without Jim's support and signing authority - monies required to support the initiatives will be delayed. Further, will Jim's lack of on-site presence affect the perceptions of others in the company in a negative manner?

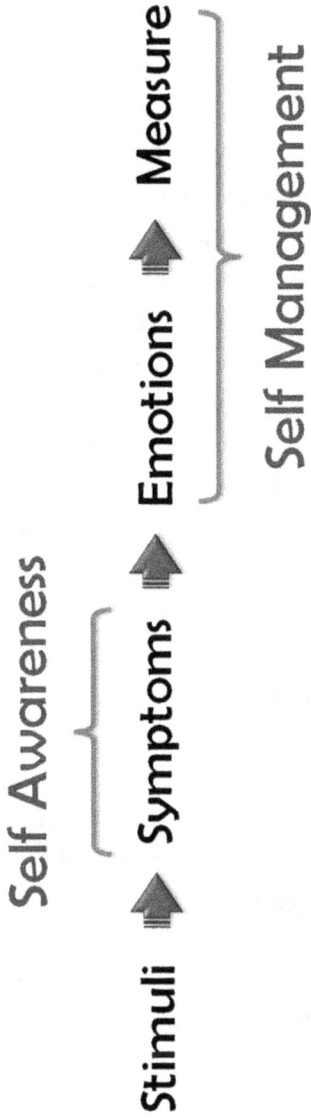

Figure 5: From self-awareness to self-management

This causes a number of biological actions which Rob immediately realizes may perpetrate a number of negative emotions.

Rob's social awareness alarm bells begin to ring. He notices a number of verbal cues telling him that something is wrong. Being an emotionally intelligent observer, Rob seeks to find out what is troubling Dan. As an emotionally intelligent practitioner, Rob measures the consequence of any emotional turmoil that may ensue and uses such information to re-think his actions. He asks himself, "If I let my emotions get the better of me, will it potentially lead to behaviors that can have a negative outcome?" Rob comes to a mental stop, begins to breathe therapeutically, and starts to think through things. If the emotion is strong Rob will need to channel his energies in a manner that expresses his potentially negative behavior until his biological actions subside.

When I channel, I typically like to work on my computer and craft a letter. Since my life history has a strong scientific disposition, any expressed comments are thoroughly reviewed. This forces me to activate my thinking process so that I can spend less time reacting on emotion, hence improving my "self-management." In Rob's case, he ends the phone conservation on a positive note and tells Dan that he will speak to Jim when he gets to the office.

In many cases, there are multiple circumstances creating emotional instability. For example, Rob's travel back to work from his off-site meeting may be a stressful experience that leaves him frustrated, yet, externally, he appears fine to everyone back at the office. However, before his meeting with Dan, suppose someone says or does something that Rob typically finds mildly bothersome sets him off into an emotional outburst. In this case, Rob's "emotional glass" is already partially full and it does not take much to overflow. To be emotionally intelligent practitioner we need to practice: stop, breathe, think and, if appropriate, channel if we hope to improve our self-management skills and assure our emotional glass does not overflow.

During his meeting with Dan, Rob realizes that he could easily adopt the negative opinions being discussed at that moment with Dan. If Rob does not put a stop to it, his own life history will take over and he will soon begin to share the same opinions Dan is expressing, thereby being fully drawn in to Dan's emotional dilemma. Rob quickly measures the consequence of this. The result will cause an enormous level of frustration among all three parties. Rob concludes that this would result in emotionally destructive behaviors and accusations leading to unproductive time trying to repair fractured relationships. The result will delay timelines and taint the business process improvement initiative.

We often find ourselves working with other individuals where each individual behaves in a manner that is the result of a circumstance. The behavior or stimuli we experience may affect us in an inappropriate manner. When that happens, we need to analyze the circumstances that motivate other people to behave the way they do. The first step is to effectively take notice of the stimuli or behavior of other people. This will improve social awareness and provide valuable insight. Such insight may be used to address the circumstance(s) in an effective manner and improve the emotional stability of the individual and/or between the members of the team, thereby improving relationship management. This chain of events is illustrated in Figure 6.

In our example, the stimulus takes the form of a number of verbal cues which ultimately results in the determination that Dan, through his conversation with Rob, is frustrated with Jim's lack of assistance. As shown in Figure 6, the stimulus is where social awareness can be improved. To become emotionally intelligent observers, we need to pick up on the non-verbal and verbal stimuli other people may be projecting.

Although Rob cannot directly "feel" the sensations Dan is experiencing, Rob is well trained to recognize facial expressions, body posture, and tone of voice. Together they communicate the emotions people may be experiencing. Rob realizes he needs to understand the root cause of the circumstance bringing about Dan's concerns with the executive in question. Only in this manner can he hope to facilitate a solution. Rob communicates his desire to assist Dan, and becomes an active participate in resolving his particular issues. Rob points out that Jim's current behavior remains unexplained. Because the facts are unknown, prejudging Jim is inappropriate. To that end, Rob has a one-on-one meeting with Jim, the executive in question. Rob shares with Jim that in Dan's opinion Jim is not providing the appropriate time and guidance to help Dan resolve project management concerns.

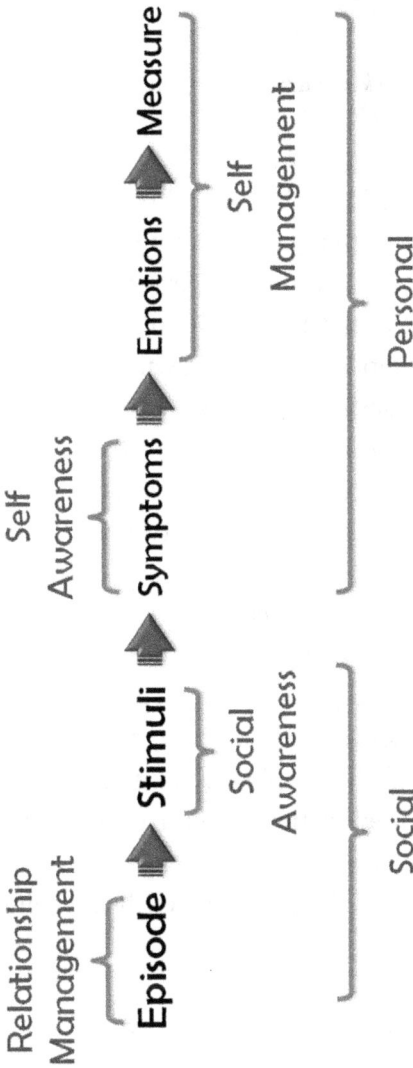

Figure 6: The emotional chain of events

In our example, Jim is the source of Dan's troubles. Rob, using his Relationship Management skills, engages Jim to determine the circumstances which triggered a Dan's emotional instability.

Stimulus: Jim's lack of participation on issues critical to Dan's project

During his meeting with Jim, Rob communicates Dan's concerns in a thoughtful manner. He describes how Jim's lack of input is causing Dan much emotional distress as a result of not being able to perform his project management duties. Rob also discusses his concerns about the overall business process improvement initiative. Thankful that Rob is bringing this to his attention, Jim talks about his own personal difficulties. Jim reveals that the company is in negotiations to be sold and will soon be purchased by another company. Although it is common knowledge that the company is for sale, the negotiations thereof are being kept confidential at the request of the purchasing company. These negotiations are being held off-site so as to avoid any potential issues that might arise if the employees of the organization knew about such negotiations. As a result of the impending sale, Jim's extensive knowledge of the operations helps facilitate the due-diligence process being conducted off-site.

Circumstance: Company Sale = Jim needs to attend off-sight due-diligence meetings

Now that the circumstance has been identified Rob has to address the root cause. In this case, the root cause is a lack of communication between Dan and Jim. Jim has failed to realize how his circumstances affect Dan's ability to perform his job effectively. Upon further investigation Rob discovers that Jim's life history supports a disposition of delegation. Since his current mandate is to facilitate the sale of the company, all other job related activities have become secondary. He has delegated tasks and responsibilities to individuals not properly prepared to handle such responsibilities for various reasons. In Jim's mind, he has assumed incorrectly that Dan and other mid-level managers can manage their particular areas without his direct guidance. Secondly, the confidentiality of the impending sale of the company has meant that Jim cannot disclose such information to many individuals within the company. Without this information, Dan has begun to formulate a poor opinion of Jim that if left unchecked could have long term negative effects on their relationship.

Root cause = *Lack of communication fostered through a need to maintain confidentiality*

As a result of analyzing the circumstance, Rob appropriately identifies the root cause and arrives at a number of conclusions. Specifically, the lack of communication between Jim and Dan needs to be addressed. The company also needs to reveal the sale of the company to its employees and Jim's relationship to such a sale. Consequently, Rob tables these issues during the company's weekly core team meeting. During this meeting, they discuss potential solutions to the root cause and decide to move forward with the following solutions.

> **Solution 1:** *Hold communication sessions weekly to discuss the progress of the sale of the company without disclosing the purchasing company*

> **Solution 2:** *Have signing authority decisions routed through Jim's administrative assistant*

As a consequence of this experience, Rob has become socially aware through his conversation with Dan. Rob understands that if Dan's frustration is left unchecked, it will continue to plague both Dan and the individuals who interact with him. Rob becomes an active member in the solution to a problem that could have caused substantial difficulty between Dan and Jim and any other people who may have been drawn into the situation. Through dialogue and an appreciation of Dan's situation, Rob is able to exercise his social awareness and relationship management skills in a number of ways.

In reviewing what happened, we see that Rob observed a number of verbal clues during his phone conversation with Dan. By meeting with Jim, Rob thoughtfully explained his encounter with Dan and revealed his experience with Dan in a truthful manner. Rob pointed out that circumstances were beyond their direct control and that assigning blame was inappropriate. This leadership approach resonated with Dan and

Jim. Rob's relationship management skills helped Dan to maintain a positive image of Jim.

Exercise

1. Try to recall an encounter that could have gone better during a meeting you have had or while interacting with another person. Try to pinpoint the stimulus triggering the biological actions within you and define the emotional response that may have resulted. Were there any non-verbal or verbal cues before the stimulus ensued?

2. Can you recall the last time you tried to understand the circumstances affecting another individual? If so, did you listen intently? Did you comprehend their circumstances? Were you a part of the process to determine the root cause?

CHAPTER SEVEN

Improve

Implement and validate solutions

Previously we discovered that the lack of communication between Jim and Dan needed to be addressed. The company also needed to communicate the sale of the company to its employees and Jim's relationship to such a sale in an effective manner. This was evidenced by Dan and Rob's phone discussion and Rob and Jim's meeting. Through dialogue, Rob remained "present" in the situation and refrained from becoming *emotionally enrolled* in a conversation with Dan. Ultimately, the circumstances and root cause were revealed, and a couple of potential solutions were identified.

> **Solution 1:** *Hold communication sessions weekly to discuss the progress of the sale of the company without disclosing the purchasing company*
>
> **Solution 2:** *Have signing authority decisions routed through Jim's administrative assistant*

The introduction of weekly communication sessions with employees will address questions and provide answers, thereby dispel rumor, since many employees had viewed Jim's absence as a bad sign for the future stability of the company. Secondly, having signing decisions routed through Jim's administrative assistant will insure that critical communications reach Jim's attention. Since Jim's administrative assistant is in regular contact with Jim, she can facilitate communication between Dan and Jim thereby assuring that appropriate issues are resolved in a timely manner.

By addressing the circumstances Rob took an active role in facilitating a solution to a number of root causes that were having an enormous impact on Dan's relationship with Jim. Such a thoughtful engagement served a number of purposes. It improved Dan's current emotional state and mitigated any potential risks that may have been encountered in the future, thereby reducing any potential effects on other people and departments within the organization.

Validating Solution No.1: Communication sessions

Holding Employee Communication Sessions is one way to address the circumstance thus discuss the perceived notion the company's future is at risk as a consequence of Jim's absence from work. During the first communication sessions, Jim expressed his loyalty to the company and its employees. His passionate and very personal speech resonated with the employees. To validate that the initial communication session went well, Human Resources solicited confidential feedback from employees through questionnaires and random one-on-one meetings with various employees. Through such a process, Human Resources came to the conclusion that questions posed by employees were adequately addressed and Jim's absence was, in fact, a good thing. Jim communicated his clear intention to negotiate the sale of the company in a manner that kept the employees interests front and center. This message resonated with many employees. They came to believe that Jim's involvement in the due-diligence process was in their best interests.

Validating Solution No.2: Signing authority process

To help facilitate this process Dan created one-page executive summaries with specific action items required of Jim. Dan forwarded these requests to Jim's administrative assistant and insured that she understood the nature of the requests so that a precise message would be communicated. The goal was to have all communication that required signing authority resolved in 24 hours. The first few attempts took longer than anticipated but were resolved within 48 hours. The failure to respond on time was traced to a technical problem with Jim's cell phone. Jim's administrative assistant quickly resolved these concerns with the Information Technology (IT) group, and the next several requests were resolved within a 24 hour time period.

Rob followed up with Dan and Human Resources, and was assured the solutions implemented were working to everyone's satisfaction. Rob's actions in bringing this issue to the core team meeting helped facilitate a few simple solutions for a problem which could have created an enormous amount of emotional instability in the workplace. Rob's skills at relationship management were instrumental in the implementation of the solution described earlier. Even though he may not have been responsible for their direct implementation, he was the catalyst.

In many circumstances, we fail to take an active lead in resolving potential issues that can cause emotional instability in the workplace. To that end, we need to be mindful of our position within the organization. We need to understand how our position and influence can effectively bring about change.

Rob has demonstrated that he is an executive who has the ability to bring issues before the right forum and then to use that forum to bring about change. People in positions of leadership must, through coaching, build their personal and social competencies. Emotional Sigma is most effective at the leadership level since such people are in positions to facilitate change affecting the workplace environment in a positive manner. In most situations, Relationship Management requires that some issues must be evaluated up the reporting ladder so that the right leadership level can affect the circumstances and their root cause(s). In most organizations, a lot of emotional instability can be traced back to a lack of self-awareness and relationship management. In their absence, the opportunity to identify the root cause and implement solutions to affect their change is missing.

Exercise

Recall a recent experience that caused a lot of emotional instability within your organization. Assume you are in a leadership position. What would you do to identify the circumstances causing this emotional instability? How could you temporarily alleviate such emotional instability? What would you do to identify the root cause(s)? Could you identify any solutions? How would you facilitate the implementation of those solutions?

CHAPTER EIGHT

Control

Monitor and sustain solutions

Given the solutions which were implemented, we must assure ourselves that they continue to sustain themselves with time. Specifically, will the communication sessions continue to answer employee questions and displace rumor? This is something Human Resources will continue to monitor.

Human Resources made sure that communication sessions were well attended. Secondly, before each communication session took place, Human Resources took a proactive role by soliciting questions from those employees who did not wish to ask such questions in public.

After each communication session, employee exit polls were conducted to solicit positive or negative comments about the usefulness of such sessions. Human Resources wanted to know whether Management's responses to questions were truthful and if their experience left them satisfied. Overall, Human Resources sought a positive exit poll rating of 85% or more. Any negative comments were addressed in follow-up communications. The first employee exit poll measured 78% positive. Over the next several sessions, the exit poll results progressively increased positively and exceeded 85%. Since Human Resources owned the communication sessions, they reported their success rate to the core team, who in turn noticed that employee morale appeared better.

Dan's relationship with Jim improved considerably. They both shared a mutual appreciation for the importance of their role and realized that the organization would benefit from their continued cooperation. Dan's project management milestones were achieved in a short time. Through Jim's administrative assistant, communication improved considerably. She absorbed new responsibilities that exercised her exceptional time management skills to Jim's benefit. Because Dan's project timelines had been achieved, he deemed this approach to project management a success.

CHAPTER NINE

Standardize

Document and Standardize Solutions

In our case study, we noted that the lack of communication between Jim and Dan needed to be addressed. The company also needed to reveal the sale of the company to its employees and Jim's relationship to such a sale. How such solutions may be used to benefit similar circumstance in the organization is an important consideration for the future.

Rob's interaction with Dan, if left unaddressed, could have potentially resulted in an enormous level of emotional instability within the workplace. By identifying the circumstance that resulted in Jim's absence from work, Rob illustrates how effective leadership may be achieved through the use of the Emotional Sigma process. Emotional stability is achieved through one's personal and social competencies to deal with potentially complex human emotions and interactions.

As we learned in the previous chapter, Human Resources established the protocol for effective communications sessions. Since a formal process did not exist, Human Resources now had an effective map and a system that could be used to communicate effectively with employees in the future. Subsequently, Human Resources implemented policies and procedures for the effective communication with employees - a new "best practice." Once the sale of the company concluded, the controlling company adopted this best practice across all business units.

Secondly, the process employed by Rob to communicate with Dan and Jim became a model for other executives. Since their roles were best utilized developing and implementing strategies and setting the future direction for the organization, their time spent dealing with daily issues would hamper their ability to realize the envisioned future state of the organization. To that end, the executives' administrative assistants were utilized effectively to filter information that had previously taken them away from their core responsibilities.

CHAPTER TEN

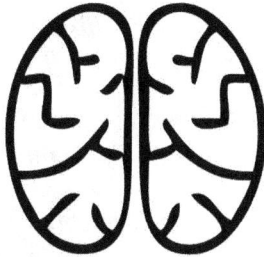

Integrate

Integrate Emotional Sigma into Leadership Coaching

The key learning outcome as a consequence of Rob's interaction with Dan and Jim was his ability to:

a. **Resist** *being emotionally enrolled into Dan's emotional instability.*

b. **Establish** *a sense of shared purpose with Dan thereby communicating that he understood Dan's frustration.*

c. **Engage** *Jim thoughtfully in a discussion to discover the circumstances feeding Dan's frustration.*

d. **Communicate** *to the core team the potential consequences of these circumstances on the organization and initiate discussions that identified solutions.*

e. **Follow-up** *with implemented solutions to validate their effect in changing the original circumstances.*

f. **Create** *"Best Practices" from this situation for the whole organization. "My team members were not up to the challenge."*

The "integrate" phase enhances organizational leadership by adopting Emotional Sigma to support overall leadership and human performance in the workplace. Integrating the learning outcomes as case studies within the Emotional Intelligence Leadership Coaching Cycle provides concrete examples of typical situations that were resolved effectively.

The basic interaction between people is an incredibly important but often largely ignored process. Organizations focus enormous amounts of money improving manufacturing or transactional processes in an effort to achieve financial stability, yet such organizations often neglect human processes. We need to address the interactions between people within the work environment. The literature clearly demonstrates that improving these interactions has an enormous effect on the financial stability of an organization. Organizations need to integrate the Emotional Sigma process in an effort to improve human processes and interactions. To that end, organizations can achieve improved financial stability and predictability.

Using the Emotional Sigma process, organizations and individuals have the ability to address emotional instability in a scientific manner. Emotional Sigma is based on the Six Sigma model for breakthrough improvement. It views an individual's emotional intelligence as an abstract mathematical equation where y emotional stability = f circumstances (x's root causes). In this case, "y" represents the 'emotion' and the "x's" represent the variables or 'root causes' that manifest the emotion "y". Lastly, "f" represents the circumstances. We must investigate the circumstances in order to identify the root cause(s) if we wish to facilitate a positive change in the emotion "y."

Typically, Emotional Sigma coaching should start at the leadership level. As each individual has his or her Emotional Sigma measured and participates in the Emotional Sigma coaching process, an organization will quickly develop a repository of information about the approaches and methods used to facilitate improvement in emotional stability. Such information can be analyzed to determine the frequency of problems experienced in the organization.

Increasing our capacity to deal with emotional instability in a more effective way requires that we increase our emotional skills through the Emotional Sigma process.

Organizations which can achieve a high degree of emotional stability can more effectively implement business strategies and achieve a greater degree of business process stability. The result will support a financially stable and predictable organization.

CHAPTER ELEVEN

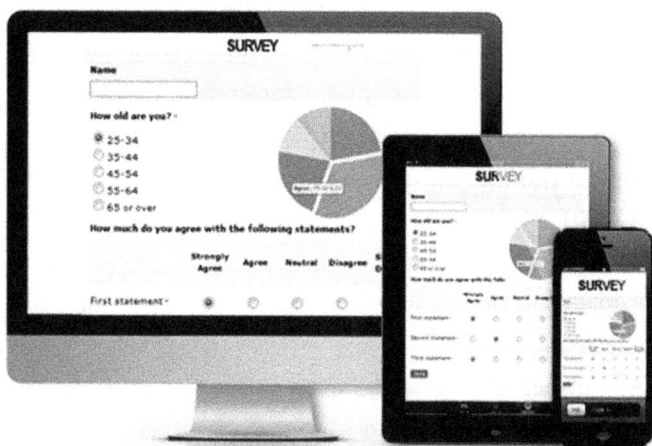

Emotional Sigma Survey

A critical element of the Emotional Sigma coaching cycle is to have an individual's current level of Emotional Sigma assessed. In this manner, coaching can be specifically targeted toward those areas of deficiency while those areas of strength can be further strengthened. Through the Emotional Sigma Survey one's Emotional Intelligence may be measured and benchmarked against others.

The Emotional Sigma Survey is a test-based instrument. It is designed to address the two emotional intelligence dimensions: Personal Competency and Social Competency. Within each of the dimensions, there are the additional categories of Self-Awareness and Self-Management along with Social Awareness and Relationship Management respectively. For each of the four categories, a number of questions are asked. The questions are specifically designed to measure each category, thereby developing an overall measure of Emotional Sigma. The questions are equally applicable to a variety of working environments.

A number of evaluators are required to assure a balanced score. As shown in Figure 7, the evaluators are a group that should have a relationship with the individual for whom the survey is intended. Collectively, there are five critical interactions an individual can have with other people. They are: "suppliers", "customers", "superiors", "subordinates", and "co-workers". A minimum of two people should be selected for a total of ten evaluators. By selecting an equal number of evaluators who have a unique relationship to the individual for whom the survey is intended, an unbiased opinion may be derived. Additional evaluators may be selected; however, try to select an equal number of evaluators. The person for whom the survey is intended normally selects his or her evaluators. I usually like to suggest a total of 20 evaluators take part in the assessment. The survey is completed on-line.

The candidate being assessed should complete a self-assessment. It helps the candidate understand the process and involves them in the process. It also provides the opportunity to examine any major differences between the survey candidate's self-perception and the other evaluators' perceptions of the candidate. It provides a consistency check for the analysis activity.

The scores are tabulated and a report is published on an Emotional Sigma scale. A higher score indicates strength; a low score points to a weakness.

Using this assessment and the Emotional Sigma process described earlier, an organization can improve leadership and human performance in the workplace.

Final thoughts...

Today, Six Sigma candidates must learn how to become successful change agents. To achieve this, Six Sigma programs need to screen candidates on two levels. First, do they have the emotional disposition to achieve breakthrough improvements in Emotional Sigma? Secondly, do they have the requisite skills to acquire and apply knowledge to create innovative business solutions?

In large organizations, where the candidate pool is substantial, I like to survey candidates for their Emotional Sigma and knowledge acquisition/application skills. This process insures that the candidates can reach their fullest potential and the organization utilizes such people to deliver innovation.

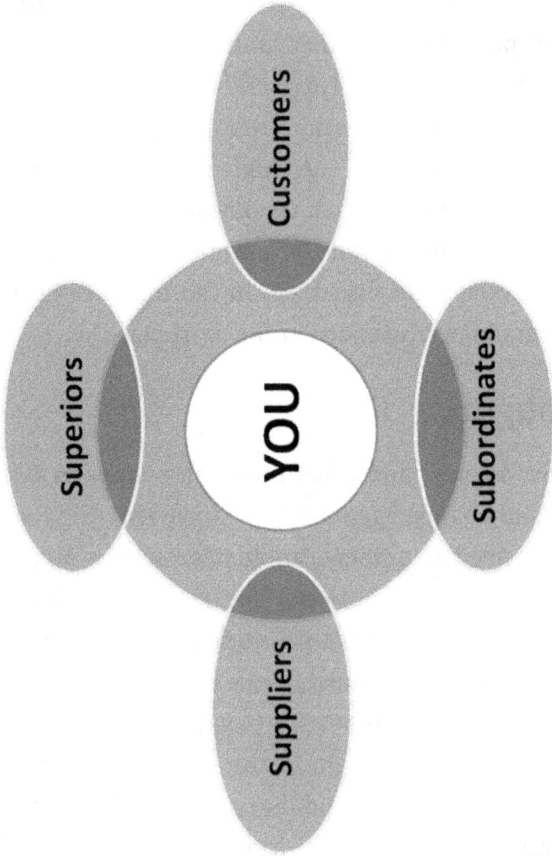

Figure 7: Critical Working Relationships – Select minimum of 2 responders for each type of working relationship

Once suitable candidates have been selected, the Six Sigma educational processes should also include Emotional Sigma coaching along with typical Six Sigma coaching. The results will produce change agents who have a comprehensive mix of technical and social skills, providing remarkable leadership potential.

Emotional Sigma is a critical element for Six Sigma Champions. Since these individuals are in leadership positions, their ability to work with people and teams effectively is critical. Not only should Champions have the technical skills to recognize organizational problems and identify the appropriate projects, they must realize that such projects are completed through people who apply the DMAIC process to such problems. A Champion's ability to work with people in the workplace is important. Finally, Champions must also standardize and integrate best practices across the organization. To that end, working with cross functional teams requires the use of Emotional Sigma to optimize team performance.

Figures

Tables

Bibliography

1.   Jack Mayer et al., "Perceiving Affective Content in Ambiguous Visual Stimuli: A Component of Emotional Intelligence," Journal of Personality Assessment 54 (1990): 772-81. See also: Jack Mayer and Peter Salovey, "The Intelligence of Emotional Intelligence," Intelligence 17 (1993): 4333-42. See also: Jack Mayer and A. Stevens, "An Emerging Understanding of the Reflective (Meta) Experience of Mood," Journal of Research in Personality 28 (1994): 351-73.

2.   Sigal Barsade, Andrew Ward, Jean D. F. Turner, and Jeffrey A Sonnenfeld, "To Your Heart's Content: The Influence of Affective Diversity in top Management Teams," Administrative Science Quarterly 45 (2000): 802-836.

3.   Peter J. Jordan, Neal M Ashkanasy, Charmaine E.J. Hartel, and Gregory S. Hooper, "Working Emotional Intelligence: Scale Development and Relationship to Team Process Effectiveness and Goal Focus," Human Resources Management Review 12, (2002): 195-214.

4.   Ibid.

5.   Daniel Goleman, Richard Boyatzis, and Annie McKee, Primal Leadership: Learning to Lead with Emotional Intelligence (Boston: Harvard Business School Press, 2004): 14.

6.   Antonio Domasio, Descartes' Error: Emotion, Reason, and the Human Brain (New York: Avon Books, 1994). See also: Antonio Damasio, "Fundamental Feelings," Nature (2001): 413, 781. See also: Antonio Damasio, The Feeling of What Happens: Body and Emotion in the Making of Consciousness (New York: Harcourt Brace, 1999).

7.   Carlos A. Estrada, Alice M. Isen, and Mark J. Young, "Positive Affect Facilitates Integration of Information and Decreases Anchoring in Reasoning Among Physicians," Organizational Behavior and Human Decision Processes, 72-1 (1997): 117-135. See also: Carlos A. Estrada, Alice M. Isen, and Mark J. Young, "Positive Affect Improves Creative Problem Solving and Influences Reported Source of Practice Satisfaction in Physicians," Motivation and Emotion 18-4 (1994): 285-299.

8.   Sigal Barsade, Andrew Ward, Jean D. F. Turner, and Jeffrey A Sonnenfeld, "To Your Heart's Content: The Influence of Affective Diversity in top Management Teams," Administrative Science Quarterly 45 (2000): 802-836.

9.   Alice M. Isen, Kimberly A Daubman, and Gary P. Nowicki, "Positive Affects Facilitates Creative Problem Solving," Journal of Personality and Social Psychology 52-6 (1987): 1122-1131.

10. Daniel Goleman, Richard Boyatzis, and Annie McKee, Primal Leadership: Learning to Lead with Emotional Intelligence (Boston: Harvard Business School Press, 2004): 39.

11.   Daniel Goleman, Emotional Intelligence: Why It Can Matter More Than IQ (Bantam, 1995): 19.

12.   David R. Caruso, The Emotionally Intelligent Manager (Jossey-Bass, 2004): 109.

13.   Ibid., 96.

14.   Ibid., 91.

About the Author

Andrew Milivojevich is widely recognized and cited in many publications as an expert in business process improvement and leadership development. He is the architect of the *FiXiT Protocol* and *Emotional Sigma*. Andrew is also the author a co-author to the best-selling text on Experimental Development called *Quality by Experimental Design*.

Mr. Milivojevich is a Professional Engineer and Fellow of the American Society for Quality (ASQ). When elected as an ASQ Fellow, he had achieved professional distinction and pre-eminence in the theory, education, application, and management of Quality. Mr. Milivojevich was cited for his exemplary work advancing Quality and Six Sigma; for being a champion of innovation through statistical methods; and for being a promoter of Experimental Development. He continues to maintain certification with the ASQ as a Certified Quality Engineer and Six Sigma Black Belt.

Currently, Mr. Milivojevich is the President of *The Knowledge Management Group* (*TKMG*). As a distinguished consultant to companies about the world, he serves his clients in their mission to improve productivity and enhance leadership. He has worked with senior executive teams, technical communities, and personally trained leaders and practitioners throughout the world.

EMOTIONAL SIGMA | 98

Besides his duties with **TKMG,** Mr. Milivojevich served on the Board-of-Directors of Autism 360 in New York. He has also served on the Advisory Board at the Center for Quality and Applied Statistics in the College of Engineering at the Rochester Institute of Technology. Mr. Milivojevich also served on the Continuous Improvement Advisory Council to Revenue Canada's Scientific Research and Experimental Development program.

In business, Mr. Milivojevich held several senior management and executive positions where he was responsible for the development, leadership, and implementation, of various continuous improvement systems. In all cases, his activities focused on the creation of world-class improvements in leadership, product quality, process performance and overall productivity.

In academia, Mr. Milivojevich served as an adjunct professor with Niagara College, Ryerson University, University of Toronto, and Conestoga College. He has taught courses in the Design and Analysis of Experiments and lectured on various productivity topics such as Work Simplification, Statistical Process Control, and Six Sigma to name a few.

Mr. Milivojevich completed his undergraduate studies in aeronautical and mechanical engineering at Ryerson University. He received his Masters of Science degree in Quality and Applied Statistics from the College of Engineering at the Rochester Institute of Technology.

Significant professional contributions include the creation of the **FiXiT Protocol - The 5 Step Process to Defect Reduction** used by companies throughout the world.

In addition, Mr. Milivojevich has authored several research articles in the fields of leadership, statistical methods, automotive engineering, and autism spectrum disorder. His research efforts in the automotive industry advanced the concepts of Automotive Seating Comfort globally. He also co-authored a substantial text book on the application of experimental design and inferential statistics. The book is entitled *"Quality by Experimental Design"*. Recently, Mr. Milivojevich published *Emotional Sigma - The 8 Step Process to Emotionally Intelligent Leadership*. Emotional Sigma leverages the discipline of Six Sigma to improve Emotional Intelligence so workplace professionals can lead their teams to positive business outcomes faster.

Mr. Milivojevich is an active speaker. He is frequently retained as a keynote presenter for industry symposiums and prestigious functions.

CONTACTING THE AUTHOR

Please feel free to share your thoughts and experiences. While I cannot respond to all emails, I will no doubt enjoy hearing from my readers.

Andrew Milivojevich
andrew@andrewmilivojevich.com

Emotional Sigma Roadmap

Emotional Sigma

The 8 Step Process to Emotionally Intelligent Leadership
For Executives, Managers, Business Professionals & Team Leaders

To learn more visit:
andrewmilivojevich.com/emotional-sigma

RECOGNIZE
symptoms that suggest
positive or negative behavior

DEFINE
emotions that create the
desired/undesired state

MEASURE
the consequences of
acting on emotions.

CONTROL
emotional outcomes
in a positive way

IMPROVE
the current
emotional state

ANALYZE
emotional episodes
objectively

STANDARDIZE
methods used to
manage future
emotional episodes

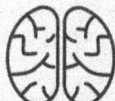

INTEGRATE
emotional lessons
into the leadership
coaching cycle

ASSESSMENT
WHAT'S YOUR
EMOTIONAL SIGMA?

TAKE THE SURVEY!

brough to you by:

#1 andrewmilivojevich.com

Emotional Sigma Survey

Take the 5 minute Self-Assessment - It's Free!

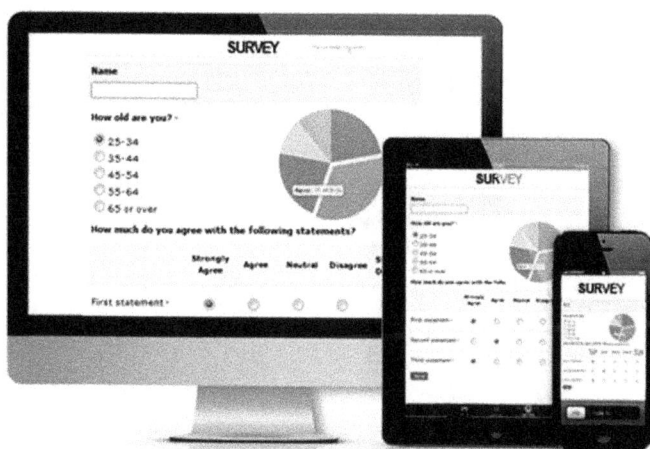

https://andrewmilivojevich.com/essbook

Use the Code: essbook

Download Resources

Download Support Documents Used in this Book

https://andrewmilivojevich.com/esdocuments

www.ingramcontent.com/pod-product-compliance
Lightning Source LLC
Chambersburg PA
CBHW070939210326
41520CB00021B/6970